I FALL TO PIECES

Copyright © 2018
Blind Dog Press
All Rights Reserved
Manufactured in Australia

Cover art © Kate Simpson

ISBN 978-0646-990-798

I FALL TO PIECES

Glenn W Cooper

for Brulee

"All angels are dangerous."
- RILKE

Contents

Is This Happiness? 11
Cure 12
Born to Die 13
All the Reasons 14
Let Yourself 16
Shades of Cool 17
An Unusual Girl 18
Critics 19
And That's the Way It Is 20
How a Song Happens 21
Ride 22
Flamingos 23
Pretty When You Cry 24
Matchmaker 25
Something Other 27
Salvatore 28
Please 29
Nothing Specific 30
Petty Thief 32
Divine 33
Butterfly 34
Horizons 35
Song 36
Heat 37
God Knows I Tried 38
Flowercrown 39
Inkblot 40
Lana and Lou 41
when i fall to pieces 42
What I Imagine Is Under Your Bed 43
Balm 44
Ultraviolence Album Cover 45

3 Fragments   46
13 Beaches   47
Real   48
Your Journals 49
The Blackest Day   51
Bel Air 52
Lust for Life   53
To Ponder   55
Untethered   56
Thirst 57
Twice, Now   58
Those Girls Who Throw Their Underwear 60
If   61
Umbrella   62
12 Possible Lines for a New Song   63
Life Is Elsewhere   64
Oh!   66
On Stage   67
Not So Much 68
You Paint Your Nails Black 69
Scarborough Fair   70
Selfie 71
Shameless   72
Sizzling Like a Snail   73
Strange Weather   75
Terrence Loves You 76
The Two of Us   77
Dead Weight 78
Darkness Is a Friend 79

Is This Happiness?

However wide the world
our longing is always wider.
From city to city, pole to pole.
Hemispheres of unmade beds.
A river of unchained tears.
Seek, find, seek again.
This is our fate, our cruel world.
Only when we finally
understand that in seeking
we will never find, will we
be able to find what we
have neglected to seek.

Cure

Every song
a fresh wound
that only
singing
can heal.

Born to Die

you did so well
not to die
though with every
fiber of your pretty
being i know
you wanted to

but you see
rebellion can take
the most unexpected
form

and you aren't
always the one
to control it.

All the Reasons

Impatient for something you
cannot describe you
strum an acoustic guitar
run your slender fingers across
the minor keys of a piano.
There is a melody

but it eludes you. Inside
that melody there is another
and it is this one
that you seek
beyond
the transparent surface.
You will have to go down

deeper to find it. Outside
a platinum sun
is shredding a blue sky.
Trees shimmer
in a hot wind. The faces
of friends and other strangers
call to you across widening
distances.

Your desperate fingers
push deeper into
the strum and thrum,
the suicidal cycle of
remembering
and forgetting.

All the reasons for living
are locked inside
that melody.

Let Yourself

Let yourself grow
young and beautiful.
Live your life
in reverse.

Forget the illusion
of progress –
it's a trap.

I write these lines
at 4 a.m., not
knowing if
I've just woken up
or am yet to go
to sleep.

Is there any difference?

It's the same lesson.

Let yourself grow
young and beautiful.

Shades of Cool

Captive on this page
you are singing in my poem

your siren song

words carved in breath
for he who calls

for you and
no one else.

Those high notes
like the whistling
of impossible birds

in impossible trees

on this blue, blue day.

An Unusual Girl

"… with no fixed personality."

You take a little
from here
a little from there.

The most desirable bits.
Or maybe
the bits that somehow
serve you best at the time,

like leaves
falling
upon
leaves
till
they form a mountain.

It starts with an absence
or an abscess

and ends with a voice
that calls from
inside another voice

a name you may
recognize
only
in passing.

Critics

"Prohibit sharply the rehearsed response." – Auden

Fuck 'em.
Don't give 'em what they want.
Be like Dylan.
Find your inner Judas.
Play too loud.
Play too soft.
Reinvent yourself
over and over again.
Arrange your moods
alphabetically and
then shuffle them again
for no good reason.
Push your dress way up high.
Moan.
Play with your back
to the audience.
Play with yourself.
Lie in interviews.
Refuse interviews.
Spit on stage.
Smoke.
Be inscrutable.
Say one thing
but mean another.
Laugh in their face.
Wear a t-shirt that says:
"Slippery When Wet".

And That's the Way It Is

She's gone. So it will be another day,
another night of listening to Lana Del Rey
alone. How distant those other times
now seem – singing along in the car or
on my bed, her sounding better than me,
Lana sounding much better than the both of us
yet still something magical in the fusion
of voices, of hearts and lives entangled
of the great unknowable cosmic unfolding.

Loneliest are those who have never sung.
Lonely still, those who have.

How a Song Happens

You smear
a white page
with red
lipstick

not so much
that you
don't have space
to write
lyrics

but enough to
make someone
think
an accident
has occurred

and in a way
it has

-- but only
if you get it

right.

Ride

"Been trying hard not to get into trouble
But I, I've got a war in my mind." – Lana Del Rey.

The war in your mind is not
for you to fight –
stand back. Observe. Study
your own thought
from afar.

Everything is just as it is
supposed to be.

Time does nothing
else
but carve us
into our true shape.

The smoke you see is not
from the battle
in your mind
but just
from your cigarette.

Blow smoke rings.

Tumble
through them.

Flamingos

Your fascination with those pink
flamingos is a mutual thing.
I see them sometimes
standing on one leg at low tide,
eyeing your body as you lay
preening, brushing, smoothing,
warming yourself in the hot sand –
their big eyes keen and kind,
their bills lazily raking
the surf for those small fish,
so sweet, so tender.

Pretty When You Cry

The deeper the hurt
the prettier you cry.
Someday your tears
will be on display
at the Louvre or
the Smithsonian.

Matchmaker

Sometimes I like to play imaginary
matchmaker. Hook you up with various
men who might have had a ghost
of a chance of keeping you
interested. Like, say, Richard Hell,
circa 1974 before the drugs had
fully kicked in and he was burning
with poetry and embryonic punk rock,
all ripped t-shirts and spikey hair.
Or maybe Neil Young in '69, crazed
with electricity, churning out
three or four classic songs a day like
it was nothing. I can see you running
your hands through Neil's rivers of long,
black hair, kicking back at the ranch,
singing sweet harmony to his heart-
breaking falsetto. Or what about
Tom Petty? Jesus! – what a couple
you would have made: his real life
American girl, free fallin' together
through the coke-soaked eighties.
But it's Dylan I think about the most.
Mid-60s amphetamine king Dylan,
to be exact. Word alchemist Dylan.
Dylan of the Cuban heels and drainpipes,
staying up all night writing songs with
15 verses and no chorus. Just imagine
him clapping eyes on you for the first
time, maybe in the Chelsea or else
the Savoy, London, 1966. He'd have
knocked everyone over to get to you.
He likes the crazed types. Gypsy girls.

Witchcraft and fortune telling.
I can see him sidling up to you, already
dreaming of that 20-minute masterpiece
that just might match the image of those
roses caught between your thighs
that you sing about in *Honeymoon*.

Something Other

Some of your songs remind me
of that same vague sense of longing
you feel when you wake up into
a rainy day. You turn onto your
back and put your hands behind
your head. As the rain gets heavier,
you close your eyes. You can feel it
beating against the back of your
eyelids. Grief for something
you cannot name, consumes you.
You have loved and felt the absence
of love and decided the two are
interlocked. You have woven
synchronicities till your fingers
ached, tied loose threads into fates.
Names. Faces. Places. In devastating
sheets of wetness they blow through
your mind. Memories are something
other than the things we have lived.

Salvatore

Eat
your hunger
while you
work on
your tan.
Let soft
ice-cream pool
in the bottom
of the bowl.
Always
your lips
must be in
a perpetual state
of desiring.
Shadow for
your shade,
summer rain
of your
concealed
self.

Please

The Lana you see in the mirror –
tell me, is she always familiar to you, as you?
Or does she sometimes appear
as though in a dream –
blurred around the edges, imprecise,
staring from inside a contextless background,
touching one perfectly manicured
nail to the glass, as if to say,
"Please, please release me"?

Nothing Specific

For this
poem
I don't want
to write
about your sex
life, your
old boyfriends,
your old life,
your alleged and
sometimes self
proclaimed
craziness.
There's
enough of that
already.
I don't want any
of that
in this poem.
Because we
are more
than our
actions, more
than the sum
total of
the things
that happen
to us,
occasionally
there should be
a poem
that says nothing
specific about

its subject,
like a glass
of water says
nothing
about a river.
Let this be
that kind
of poem.

Petty Thief

"I stole your bible, I stole your gun."
             -- Lana Del Rey

You stole the ocean from the bathtub
& the blood's furious circulation
You stole the going before it was ever coming
You stole night away from day
    & from day
    the sun's invisible shadow
You stole death from the damp cemetery
    & made it life again
You stole the tongue's desire
You stole hunger from the mouth
    & the ache from the head
You stole the hopelessness of one thing
    & made real
the hope of another
You stole the flower's germination
You stole the planet's electric current,
the tide's undulations
    & the moon's slow progress
    around your body
You stole the alcohol from sobriety
You stole sleep from the night's coma
You stole the aroma of forests
You stole the found in the disappeared
    & the smoke from the cigarette
You stole the turbulence from the wind
You stole the completion from finished
    & the target from the arrow
    the lips from the kiss
    the obscurity from the dream.

Divine

"I wasn't crazy / I was divine." – Lana Del Rey

the only
difference

between
myself

and a mad-
man is that

I am
not mad,

Salvadore Dali
once said.

your line
from

I Can Fly
made me

think
about that

statement in a
different way.

Butterfly

That butterfly on your lips
let it linger there
a little longer.
Its wings beat for you
and you alone.
Let it drink. I imagine
the moisture of your lips
could sustain such a creature
for a lifetime. Or
at least until the night
arrives and it must alight
to that place where it is
that butterflies go to sleep.
But forget that.
I'd rather it stay
where it is, oblivious
to time and distance
the sun's setting or
the moon's rising.
This is the true
butterfly effect – one
delicate creature gently
resting on another, no
storm from flapping wings
no oblique consequence.

Horizons

Something about
horizons
always
makes me
think of you.
Something about
false endings
and the lure
of falling into
new beginnings
devoid
of gravity
and the things
that keep us
grounded.
We put one foot in
front of the other
but never get any
closer –
our feet heavy
with too little
hope and
too much
destination.

Song

Song falls upon song
like cloud entering cloud

new shapes to ponder

each of them a perfect
mould for my slow
to evaporate sadness.

Heat

Certain contexts I can't
imagine you in. Like
snow skiing or even walking
in Paris on a rainy day.
The images just don't fit.
No. I can only picture you
in hot climates under sunny
skies. In shades. Preferably
poolside in a too-small bikini
sipping a cold drink. Your
natural habitat. Maybe
it's the heat you radiate that melts
the idea of snow, of cool things.

god knows i tried

it's important to know
if you're the bird or the cage.
all your voices sing at once –
a spell to dissolve bars.
songs are a diagnosis.
one way to sing is to listen
to how others are doing it
and not do it like that.

poetry is the smoke
but never
the
fire,
just as song is the hope
but never
the
promise.

Flowercrown

I imagine flowers growing
around your heart,
maybe wild roses –
bud nudging ventricle,
valve among the thorns.
The ceaseless blooming.
The opening and closing
of petals mixed with blood,
in a steady internal
rain. Melancholy music
in the lilting rhythm
of your veins.

inkblot

your
black
nails
chipped
into
irregular
shapes
like
tiny
inkblots
and
as
with
most
things
we
see
in
them
whatever
we
want
to
see,
right?

Lana and Lou

Sometimes I wonder what your favorite
Lou Reed song is. I'm guessing it might be
Sweet Jane or *I'll Be Your Mirror*, though,
of course, you namecheck *Walk on the Wild Side*
in *Born to Die*. And you have a song called
Heroin. Actually, I can easily imagine you
and Lou together in, say, the late sixties or early
seventies ... all leather and fur, popping pills.
Drinking at Max's Kansas City. Holding court.
You'd have suited him better than icy Nico.
You'd have added sweetness to his sour.
Nico and Lou were too much alike. Too much
of the one thing. You'd have balanced things out.
You sing of doomed love but Nico was just
doomed. Lou always knew it. You'd have sung
her songs perfectly, or the songs Lou wrote
for her to sing. I wonder if you'd have gotten
along with Nico? Probably not. Nico didn't
get along with anyone. Or as someone who
knew her said in the "Nico: Icon" film:
"No one loved Nico and Nico loved no one."
That's no way to live. Being born to die is one
thing but being dead while living is another.
Poor Nico. Poor Lou. I heard you were
supposed to meet him on the day he died.
That's beautiful. Poetic. Truth is always
stranger than friction. I really wish you'd
cover *Sweet Jane* on your next record.
I can hear your voice singing, "Heavenly
wine and roses seem to whisper to her
when he smiles." Can you hear it, too, Lana?

when i fall to pieces

i do it one
atom
at a time

hoping my
disintegration
to be so
thorough

and
complete

but
to
last

such a
long time

that you might
not even
notice

that I'm
gone.

What I Imagine Is Under Your Bed

… a shoebox filled with
ticket stubs
hotel napkins
rail passes from forgotten journeys
Polaroids
dried flowers
a pet rock from the early '90s
feathers
a lens cap
receipts for items you cannot remember buying
Valentine's day cards (received)
Valentine's day cards (unsent)
a hair ribbon
a pink marker pen run dry
school reports that hint at unfulfilled potential
charcoal sketches that come off on your hands
a seashell
a piece of white lace hacked from a larger piece
       of white lace
a guitar pick
business cards advertising services you no longer require
yellowed newspaper clippings
buttons
a plastic ring
and a little toy airplane missing its landing gear.

Balm

Time is your little slut
heartbreak your whore

Quick! Quick! –
your red lips weep.

Cake them with words –
a balm for every malady.

You know your
impatient perfection
won't wait forever

to be kissed.

Ultraviolence Album Cover

Someone said you had perfected the art
of looking sad while smiling.
Yet I can see not even a trace
of a smile here. Perhaps something
the inverse of that.
A mouth thrashed by falling tears.
The look of someone who is for
today at least done with cameras.
The distressing endlessness
of flowing with the current, of being
swept along without sail or rudder.
Your dark eyes are a homage
to a certain type of doomed love,
usually found in nineteenth century
French poetry or in the songs
of sultry Francoise Hardy – eyes
of the beaten storm, of dripping clouds,
eyes that cannot look beyond waiting.

3 Fragments

Flicking cigarette ash into empty coffee cups, fingers conduct this late-night orchestra, flourish and finality, the sweep of the frantic galaxy overhead – two half-written songs in crumpled balls at your feet.

Sheets twisted into sleepless knots, a pillow damp with tears, sex and ex rejects, the neighbors all night pound their shitty music, rain in squalls against the window – pretty bruises the color of lilacs on your thighs.

Eyes reddened by too much reality, a melody is no remedy, this is only a version of life and crying is mostly muscle memory – your mouth caked with unsaid words.

13 Beaches

In hard times
just watch how

those waves
you see
breaking over
the rocks

immediately

repair themselves

only to begin
again

over and over.

Real

*"Oh my god, she's real!" – overheard at a
LDR concert as she walked on stage.*

or at least
an approximation

of
such

for how can we
ever really know

flesh beyond
the machinations

of the eye?
even touch is

subject to
an agreement

between
finger and brain

with so much
capable of being

lost in
the final translation.

Your Journals

The pages of your journals,
I imagine, bear the mark
of the poet, the songwriter,
with many crossed out words
and passages. Underlines
in red ink. Some of the writing,
I bet, runs vertically along
the margins – late thoughts,
additions, addendums.
Your handwriting is neat –
a shrink might say this is one
way you have of regaining
control. Something within
your grasp. It could be so,
though I have little time
these days for psychology
or anything that probes
the minds of men and women
for a deeper understanding.
Mostly things are just as they
seem to be and beneath the
surface level mud there is only
more mud. But I don't want
to sound cynical. Not here.
Enough roses already lay strewn.
Enough ashtrays hurled in anger.
I bet you try to stay positive
in your journals, too. Reflect
on the brighter stuff. The glint
of the sun on the sand on one
of those thirteen beaches. City
lights seen from a vantage point.

Maybe descriptions of people
you meet on your travels.
Not the sad stuff. Not the stuff
that goes into the records. This
is something different, something
between yourself and yourself
that only the snow white, empty
pages of an unlined journal
could hope to understand.

The Blackest Day

The ocean gathers 'round her feet.

And then the sound
of a great tearing
of heart
of idea & inclination.

In her anguish she confuses
the love of action
with the action of love.

There is no still life.

It is the crossed-out words
that make the most impact
on the other side of the page.

Bel Air

Bel Air,
I like
your simple
little melody,
reminding me
of the songs
I would
sing to myself
as a child,
when making up
songs
while I played
in the garden
seemed a natural thing.
Picasso said he spent all
his adult life
trying to remember
how he drew
as a child, never
succeeding.
Maybe I'll spend
the rest of my
own life trying
to remember
those childhood
songs, but
until I do,
at least
I will
I have this
song.

Lust For Life

Cold Sunday afternoon listening
to *Lust For Life*.
Critics are saying you are
more outward on this record, less
inclined to navel-gaze, like
somehow that's a good thing,
that one mustn't look
inward, no no no,
everything should be about surface
level textures, fucking
fingernail deep.
Yet I don't really think this record
is outward looking at all. Sure
there's the end of America
political statement
song
and there's *Change*, but
everything else is
in keeping
with what has come
before, all that
pent up relationship stuff,
the spilled blood, the hot tears
that just won't stop
coming, the
way it's impossible to navigate
through the human
cesspool without
losing at least a little
of your sanity

and that's

exactly
how
I
like
it.

To Ponder

I like the way you confuse "I"
with your eyes. If seeing is believing,
then hope is forgetting.
The beauty in the eye is beholden.
Seeing becomes less a sense than
an obligation. Your eyes should be
no barrier to how you see yourself.
(Night is made from the shapeless things
we trip over.) Every truth is
indistinguishable from friction.
You opened your parenthesis
so casually, what was I
supposed to think?

Untethered

"There's no remedy for memory."
– Lana Del Rey.

The muddied mind of the heart sick.
Whispered things to a dreaming face.
As if all the hours of the day
formed a puzzle, something to be
pushed into shape, into form.

Rain empties into the jar, the cut
flower bends, the wind blows.

Simply adrift on this page are all
the words
                untethered.

thirst

all night long i escape
into certain songs
that remind me of other times –

like the way *Shades of Cool*
reminds me of a particular
car journey with

a certain someone in
the early evening hours,
both us flushed with love

or its close approximation,
mixed with the grief
of not knowing,

yet somehow also aware,
that this journey would be
our last, at least on this plane

of existence; Lana's voice
soaring like an angel
above the madness

of our plight,
of her tears,
my tears, our tears

all that salt reminding us
why we were so
thirsty for one another.

Twice, Now

Twice, now, I've seen you
in a dream. The first time
you were on stage. You
had the look of someone
who had pushed through
the fatigue barrier and was now
getting a second wind, playful
and sexy-tired as you romped
around the stage in your silver
mini skirt and black OTK boots.
The second time it was
poolside and you were
reading Kerouac –
Big Sur, I think it was –
coming on all bohemian
and philosophical in
your red bikini and wet hair.
I said something like, "Lana,
good and bad things arise
at the same time," to which
you – casually lighting
a cigarette – replied,
"New things are usually just
the old things rearranged."
It was impossible to argue –
you were way too beautiful
and besides, it was true.
Bored, you went back to
your book, turning the pages
with your long, aqua tipped
fingernails. Something in
the way you turned the pages

made me think of a man
suiciding off a cliff on a
rainy night in July.

Those Girls Who Throw Their Underwear at You On Stage

Forgive them,
they want only
for you to know
the sweetness
of their affection,
the unhurried scent
of their longing.

If

Lana,
If I were to write
a haiku for you,
I think I'd have to
start with your syllabic
lips: begin there
and then determine
if anything else
(unlikely)
needed to be said.

Umbrella

Think of an
umbrella
with its skin
torn
away –
the metal
skeleton
held aloft in
a futile
gesture
against the slow
but
inexorable rain.

That's how I
feel about
much of
life.

I bet you do,
too.

12 Possible Lines for a New Song

Today, my mood cannot support the weight of these sad songs

Inside this line there is another line, aching to get out

A beer yawn was all he could muster

It's cold between these pages

A full-stop's interior is a hollow ending

In absence we generate fresh affection

Are we related to the past?

Words are wands

The indecency of memory

Realism is a symptom, not a cause

Ballad of the unsent letter

When silence becomes animated, vast cacophonies bloom.

Life Is Elsewhere

"Life is elsewhere," said
Rimbaud, a poet
you might like
to check out
if you haven't
already done so.
Did all his writing
between 15 and 20
then walked
away and never
wrote another
word. Became
an explorer in
Africa and was
dead at 37.
A true rebel.
Born to die.
His most famous
pronouncement
was "I is another,"
which means
that the poet
and his words are
not the same
thing. All those
people who
think they know
you from your
songs would do well
to remember this.
"I am a spectator
at the flowering

of my
thought,"
Rimbaud also
said.
Water it.

Oh!

Pepsi-Cola never
tasted so good!

On Stage

You ask, you receive.
You give so much, yet
part of you is also
taken away.

Thus, this is a night
like no other, a night
like all others.

The stage lights do more
to conceal
than to expose.

You wear an outfit, yet
the outfit wears you.

Everything in time becomes
its inverse,

often even before
you realize it.

Not So Much

Shimmering –
not so much
dancing
as
creating
a crackling
electrical
disturbance
in the air
surrounding
your
body.

You Paint Your Nails Black

Painting your toenails,
your knees drawn up
under your chin, the soft
light from the bedroom
window falling just so.
Harmony of harmonies,
verse of verses;
moving from one toe
to the other, your hand
steady as a surgeon or
like a small child
reaching for a butterfly.

Scarborough Fair

I loved it when you sang *Scarborough Fair* on your
LA to the Moon tour. You always mispronounced it
as "*Scars*borough" but that didn't matter to anyone.
It's such a beautiful song, truly a melody to die for.
I'd had a brief but very intense relationship with
a woman who also used to sing that song. She
sang it faster than how you do it, more rollicking,
but with the same heartbreaking melody
still intact. She sent me a rough recording of it –
recorded on her phone – just the first two verses –
but enough to savor. I played it over and over.
The woman is gone now, but I have that short
recording on my iPod so that I can hear her voice
whenever I want to. I hope you keep singing
that song, Lana – it will always remind me
of that time, of her beautiful dark hair and
soulful eyes, and the way she infused everything
with a certain warm light that eviscerated
my own darkness, at least for a time.

Selfie

Cameras can only
show what's
plainly seen

the way a polygraph
can only
detect
a lie
but never
a truth.

Shameless

"Slipping on my dress in soft filter."
– Lana Del Rey

When you sing a line
      like that
it is almost impossible
for the listener not
to visualize it
for the rest
of the day.

Or at least
it's impossible for me,
   anyway.

So, when you
      sing that line
understand that
you are a shameless
disruptor
      of thought,
& a corruptor of minds!

Sizzling Like a Snail

Sometimes
it's the mis-hearings
that are the most fun, like
in *Sad Girl* I always thought
the bridge was,
"I'm not violent, baby,"
instead of "I'm on fire, baby."
It made sense to me
because the proceeding lines are,
"Watch what you say to me,
careful who you're talking to."
A threat. And then,
"I'm not violent, baby."
Not usually. But for you
I can make an exception,
if you don't
watch your mouth …

In *13 Beaches*
I thought it was
"the bar room of my mind,"
which to me is
a pretty cool image.
And in *Heroin*
I thought it was
"It's fucking hard!
It's hard!"

Ride – "Don't rape me now."

The mis-hearings tell a story, too –

maybe one just as important
as what was
originally intended –

in the same way that what we
discern from a dream is
probably just as insightful
as what the dream
was really telling us.

Strange Weather

"I can't do nothing about his strange weather."
-- Lana Del Rey

Weather is
internal, too, not
just something
to be observed
at a comfortable
distance. You
must let that
other person rain
on you, feel
their blustery changes.
As for yourself,
when you hear that thunder
rumbling from deep
within, don't cover
your ears – instead,
count the decibels!
Wear them like
a badge of
honor, feel your
whole house
shake to
the point
where it could
collapse
at any moment,
then wait
for the next
flash.

Terrence Loves You

When you thought you'd lost yourself,
you hadn't really, for the song about losing
is always the song about finding. A little
night rain at the window. Sad jazz. Trashed!
The unmade jigsaw still depicts the same scene.
Piece by piece you are put back together.
Small hands in messy rooms, fumbling.
Complicated assemblage in the flawed light.

The Two of You

Lizzie, weep for Lana
Lana, weep for Lizzie

Whether you know it
or not
you each stand
in the same hard rain

your arms folded
against the cold

your coat turned
inside out

and your eye
makeup running.

Dead Weight

Throw your flower crown to the wind.
    Let it roll, let it tumble.

        Don't miss it.

It was only a crown of thorns
    in disguise.

Darkness Is A Friend

Darkness is a friend
but you mustn't
let it get too close.
Not close enough
that it can cozy up.
Not that type
of friend.
But just so close
that you can call
on it when you need it.
Something you can use
to conceal
or to blot out
the glare.
Things can grow
in the dark, too.
Don't let anyone tell
you any differently.
And what you
cultivate in the dark
can always survive
in the light, too,
just like the dream
you have of yourself
will always survive
the reality
of what others
think you are.

www.ingramcontent.com/pod-product-compliance
Lightning Source LLC
Chambersburg PA
CBHW031210090426
42736CB00009B/862